What We're Made Of

May 2016

What We're Made Of

Poems by Lisken Van Pelt Dus

Cherry Grove Collections

For Shawna —

Happy Birthday
and best wishes for a wonderful
career in words !

— Lisken

Published by Cherry Grove Collections
P.O. Box 541106
Cincinnati, OH 45254-1106

ISBN: 9781625491831

Poetry Editor: Kevin Walzer
Business Editor: Lori Jareo

Visit us on the web at www.cherry-grove.com

Cover art:

Lawren S. Harris
Canadian, 1885–1970
"Lake Superior," c. 1923
oil on canvas
111.8 x 126.9 cm (44 x 49 15/16 in)
The Thomson Collection © Art Gallery of Ontario
AGOID.103943
© Family of Lawren S. Harris

Author photo: Hunter Andrus

Acknowledgements

Deeply felt thanks to all who have encouraged and taught me, especially the faculty and participants of *The San Miguel Poetry Week* and my fellow Crossing Paths members, as well as to the editors of the publications in which these poems first appeared, sometimes in slightly different form:

Cider Press Review:	"The Uses of Appetite"
The Comstock Review:	"Broken Things," "Toccata"
Floating Bridge Review:	"Entering the Earth"
Hard Row to Hoe:	"West Stockbridge, 1941"
Illuminations:	"Greek Time"
New Madrid:	"Becoming Double," "Lacking Wings"
qarrtsiluni:	"The Lake Isn't a Life," "The Latch Once Lifted," "Self-Portrait as Aquifer," "Visiting the Burn Unit"
The South Carolina Review:	"Disintegration"
Umbrella:	"You in this Field, Where I Have Pulled Over My Bike"
upstreet:	"Entropy," "Light"
The Warwick Review:	"In Both Hands," "No One Counting"

"The Lure of the Exotic" won an International Merit Award in *Atlanta Review*'s 2002 International Poetry Contest, and first appeared in *The Berkshire Review.*

"The Edge of Everything" and "The Queen of Hearts" each won a Special Merit Award, and "You Ask Me to Explain" was a Finalist, in *The Comstock Review*'s Muriel Craft Bailey Award Contest (2002, 2003, and 2008), and originally appeared in that journal. "The Edge of Everything" also appeared subsequently in *Umbrella*.

"Christmas in Puerto Angel" first appeared (as "Puerto Angel") in the anthology *Crossing Paths: An Anthology of Poems by Women* (Mad River Press, 2002).

"He Calls It Love" won first prize in Ledgetop Publishers' *Writing the River* Contest, and first appeared in their *Writing the River* anthology (2005).

The editors of *Cider Press Review* nominated "The Uses of Appetite" for a Pushcart Prize.

"Abundance," "Becoming Double," "Broken Things," "Disintegration," "Flight of Starlings," "Lacking Wings," "The Language of Flight," "Seam," "Lineage" (as "Self-Sufficiency"), "What You Listen To" (as "Strawberries"), and "You in this Field, Where I Have Pulled Over My Bike" appear in the chapbook *Everywhere at Once* (Pudding House Press, 2009).

"Broken Things" also appears in *Letters to the World: Poems from the Wom-po Listserve* (Red Hen Press, 2008).

For Mummy, who gave me poetry, and Bob, who sustains it.

quintessence, *n.*

1. **a.** In classical and medieval philosophy: a fifth essence existing in addition to the four elements, supposed to be the substance of which the celestial bodies were composed and to be latent in all things

   b. *Astron.* A form of dark energy that varies in time and space and has negative pressure, proposed to account for the apparent accelerating expansion of the universe as suggested by observations of some distant supernovae

- Oxford English Dictionary

Table of Contents

I – Appetite

II – Dark Energy

III – Fifth Essence

IV – From a Distance

I

Appetite

The Uses of Appetite

It requires a willingness to be broken,
to break willingly – not the rubble
of a dropped dish, the miserable
truck dangling its muffler in the yard,
the pot-holed road – but the sky

watering, the softened crocus leaves,
the branch snapped when it is more
than the tree can bear, the mountain
melting into spring. We can hold
only so much, the world tells us.

Since I'll break anyway, I may
as well be full when it happens.
I want to flood the earth with my spilling,
feel my self swell, swallow all of it:
oceans, the taste of wind dropping,

your fingers on my neck, your
husky morning voice. I want
to seep into the neighbors' house
and drink whatever love I might
find there, between slammed doors

and silent, shuttered pauses.
I want to be big like morning, long
like rivers running through chasms
to the sea. I want to be all of it,
all of you, until you burst me.

The Secret Life of Rocks

By the time you explain the mechanics of frost heaves
it's too late –

the secret's out. Rocks are alive –
unerring instinct for *up*

the lynch-pin of the argument.
We know about craving sky.

Think of exploding through the surface
from underwater –

partly you gasp for air but partly
it is the universe opening from inside

and the knowledge that we touch the earth
at only the tiniest tangent –

and still hang on. It's hard work,
but the rock nosing up by the daisies

has witnesses – us,
and the great slow blink

of night, day – our planet spinning ceaselessly
into the sun.

Entropy

To the north, the mumble of a train
grinding the long tracks beside the beaver pond.
Just south, a truck drowns it with its doppler,

but still I hear the fledgling robins squawk
indignant hunger. Wind shakes the treetops
free of rain that falls onto my page. It all falls

apart, gradually, the whole universe, or so
the scientists tell us, and I believe them,
the way I settle into home gratefully

and then spend my dreams on breaking
out, desire for what is not mine
feeding the filament of want I spin

into the air. Its shimmer tells me I'm alive.
Even if our lives are good, and sweet –
like mine, I readily admit – it's not

enough for something in us, the part
that doesn't care if it gets snared in webs
of its own making as long as it keeps

moving, like this spider, trapped
in a stickiness that only yesterday
was his survival, two legs snapped off,

free finally of function but unable
still to leave the tangle of their home.
I want it all. It hurts to lose

our energy and, worse, just in proportion
to our attraction to disorder. So time
runs down, and now the wind has stretched

all but two strands of the old web
to breaking point, and the dead spider
swings from the railing, making no sound at all.

White-Limned Morning

All morning snow, falling lightly against grey
and muffled traffic. Then just before noon

the cap on the world lifts: sky suddenly blue
and ready to go anywhere, ready to be everywhere.

In the night I woke from a dream where I was
many people, and for a little while I made some

sense of it. Then I snugged the duvet closer.
Let them go, I told myself. Now here is the sky

turning itself inside out right in front of me.
Nothing so important it can't be released –

sky bursts into blue improbability, sun
shines bright on a white-coated world.

What can I do but yearn and get on with
what has to be done. The sky can wander.

Lacking Wings

Lacking wings, we hang a lot on words,
to signal danger, love, the color
of the flight we'd like to take.
Some of mine show up in Spanish —
golondrinas, revoloteo. Sometimes I gather
swallows, hover, but these are not
the same, these flutter over
someone else's land.
                        We hear
the voices of the ones who nourish us
and the ones who threaten —
our song sparrows, our blue jays —
and learn our first words as we spin
between them.

                When the jays finally
moved on this morning to the next
neighborhood, the other birds sang
in relief. I can't transcribe
their song, but I can
tell you this:
                if I turned bird,
my wings would curve like gondolas.
I would fly into evening, vagrant
and longing, would call endlessly.

The Life Contracted

Let's speak of Javier, the guitarist, playing over breakfast at the café
just for the soul of it.

That's his sky he's under: its sun cresting the church's dome,
its dust too cold as yet to smell of much.

Soon it will smell of fire and footpaths, and his songs
will hang like echoes through the day, like the worlds I want

to keep inside me – but I'm learning that isn't possible, not really.
The only sky I can tune into is the one I'm in

and that changes. As it has to, like a bonsai tree, its
sprawl and need of pruning.

Hands grip the branches, squeeze, wrap, and cut.
In the morning a new sky will be waiting for me.

And then another. And then another.
Each a different chord. Think of the bonsai tree, forced new.

He Calls It Love

He would defend it, he says:
the right of the river to be more than one.
The slow one, murmur hushed
as the flutter of wings on stones.
The evening one, light-gatherer
like the first taste of waking from dark sleep,
body beside you radiant and surprising.
The icy one: unexpected channels
of winter moving, and the sound
of hard sex behind closed windows.
The fast one who knows only
how to leave when the rain pours in.
He would defend them all, he says,
the many ways we love.

On Your Birthday

Earth woke inverted.
The sidling sun spurted

through fog, pounced
on greening hills, announced

that it had plans for us –
Want to be luminous?

it asked. I did. I do.
And so I burn for you.

The Queen of Hearts

It wasn't berries that we had in mind –
hiding in thigh-high grasses,
nuzzling the rustling haze of summer,
nothing in our senses –

hiding in thigh-high grasses –
but each other, and the tremor of heat.
We had nothing in our senses
but the air sizzling with crickets and bumblebees,

each other, and the tremor of heat.
We submerged ourselves,
left the air sizzling with crickets and bumblebees,
entered a world dark, cool, attenuated.

We submerged ourselves,
found, to our surprise, a field of swollen strawberries
in their own world – dark, cool, attenuated
and slow like memory.

Surprise! A field of swollen strawberries –
what could we do but pick them,
side by side, slow like memory,
and take them from the meadow.

What could we do but pick them?
The tarts will be delicious, will taste
of meadow and being taken, and of
the longing gathered from our fingertips.

The tarts will be delicious. Taste
the rustling haze of summer,
the longing gathered from our fingertips –
berries, and all that we had in mind.

Self-Portrait as Aquifer

As if flesh were permeable –

      not flesh exactly, but the whole body
      we carry around,
               what we feel with –

like rock rain-sodden, permeable
channeler
          (willing, unwilling)

      of water's need
      to be going somewhere

      like me right now
      wanting to go out in the rain –

how could I have known how deep

            you would enter me?

Greek Time

It will be hot today, air expanding atom by atom
to fill the atmosphere. Everything will swell

into its largest self – roses peeled open
to their fragrant center, sky the kind of blue

that always has room for more – like the day
I entered Olympia, where crickets sang

their Greek name – *zizikas* – and I could hear,
I swear, the creak and murmur of the pine trees growing

among the discs of columns toppled in the grass.
For days, we'd trailed Dmitri round more populous sites

(always the guide was called Dmitri),
our footsteps crunch-crunching on dusty,

dutiful paths. And then Olympia –
green-shaded. Theodosius and earthquakes

had done their best to level it,
but here it was, spilling the slow scent

of centuries into the air. This was years ago,
but today: the smell of pine and laurel from my roses.

Seen and Unseen

You've spent hours arranging colors
in the garden to please me. No bouquet
is big enough and so you paint

with swaths of daisies, banks of lilies,
perfumed arrays of roses by stone walls.
We've known since we were kids

that seeing is desire, our desire seeing,
the possibilities of plastic brought to life
on living-room floors among the pictures

of the Sears & Roebuck catalogs,
the crayoned circling an early exercise
in mixing want with need, a skill

we just get better at with time.
It's never enough,
everything.
                    Our hearts surge

at the sight of an old oak tree, its
spreading branches arced
like a green fountain. Oh,

to slow down enough to see its flow....
Instead, you garden
and I exchange at least a few new words

for old ones scattered on my desk.
It's all we can do, really, like the man
in the street-sweeper, cocked

to the winter-littered curb, intent
on each grey patch of pavement. Got
to go slow. It's always in fog —

everything.

Aurora Borealis

I had only my parents' word for it: the second
successive night of Northern Lights.
They'd promised to wake me if the bright creatures
emerged again, and wake me they did –

or so they told me at breakfast. But I
didn't remember seeing the searchlights
of the northern dawn too impatient to wait
for sunrise, had slept through it, though

I'd talked and walked and had the grown-ups
fooled. Of course, the joke was still on me
so I took comfort in Grandpa's workshop,
matching hammers to their silhouettes on walls,

seduced into believing that all things
have their place – a home for every stray,
a feasting chair for every famished mouth,
and no need to search very far afield

for tools to fix things with – Ace Hardware
only twenty miles southward from the lake,
high-aisled, filled with fraction-labeled drawers
and a staccato light that hummed with male

excitement. Turned out the Northern Lights
sound something like that hardware store –
I heard them later, glissando to the stars
dimming their own harmonics in return.

I've been a sucker for the long view north
since that pajamaed night, like all the planet
seeking alignment, or a fix on my position, afraid
of missing once again what's right

in front of me. I mouth the name like prayer –
aurora, borealis – lips formed into an O
like the moon's outline or like hungriness
roaring to take in anything that fits.

Taking My Leave

The moon this week was closer
than it will be again this year,
and Venus has cast her ancient light
with particular vehemence, beacon
across an endless ocean. I give them
my heart for the taking. I give them
my taking for their heat. It's the oldest

ecstasy, an endless appetite
for fire, for the luster
of our lives, for what passes
between two bodies in a muted night,
near-silence of vibration, what feels
like sex but isn't. Think of it
like working toward a center,

peeling and turning as you might
the leaves of an artichoke, savoring
flesh against teeth, more and more
tender. Nothing remains for us to do
but circle our own selves, strip
ourselves gently open until
whatever stardust we are made of

is released. I'm taking my leave:
its tremble, its braced spine, backward
glance. I take it and swallow it,
like ice, like hard sorrows, so it travels
with me. What's left is my arrival,
perpetual, opening a gash in me
that I pour out of, each departure

a homing – so many sweet streams
run through me, so many arroyos
to fill. The closest I can come to a color
for Venus is yellow, but fire like that
is beyond all color. I arch my head back,
let the night's brightness sear me,
everything I have to give already given.

You Ask Me To Explain

Not thunderous, no hooves pounding.
Not fireworks, sirens, sparks
falling from air like petals. Not what you think,
reader, not body if by body you mean
muscle, sinew, blood pounding. I told you,
not thunder. Something you can't even hear.
Something green and yielding – not
like grass or clover – something airier,
something to do with light. I know
you don't believe me, you think there was
something I could do about it. I couldn't.
Help me, offer suggestions. If you say
it was like sunset splayed across a broad horizon
I will say, no, it was not that.
Not the infinitude of mirrored mirrors, either.
Not the cry of a wolf on the long ridge
approaching. Not terraces in sunlight, not
the astonishment of clear water in a glass,
not oysters offering pearls, not even
the sand at their source. Forgive me
my imprecision. I'm trying to explain.
It wasn't about us. It wasn't about what we call
our lives. Immeasurable. Unutterable.
Not darkness or light. Not heat or cold.
Not attached to time. It had something to do
with water, but it was also sky.
It had something to do with salt, but
it was also sweet – not like honey – harder.
It was unconsumed by its own fire. Like
physics undone, we came out larger. No,
not even that. Not tigers. Not kestrels

hovering, not the cracked-egg sky.
Outside dimension. Reader, it wasn't even
he, I, we. Are you with me? It was everything
and nothing: a knot, unassailable,
and the endless ropes of us untethered.

II

Dark Energy

Disintegration

At the first break of blue sky, the birds grew quiet.
Coincidence, of course, as the crows made clear
a moment later, but still, a silence long enough

to draw my eyes up. The triangle of soft, astonished blue
appeared like all the grace we have imagined:
forgiveness of our sins, a holy trinity, transcendence

like the pointed peaks of worshipped mountains –
Fuji, the Matterhorn, Popocatepetl – thinning
with the air into a purity beyond our grasp,

relying as we do on what we see and touch.
But we are small ourselves as any stone;
what we have been spirals behind us in a vortex

of shed electrons, detritus of what we no longer
can ever be again. It happens at every moment,
like the clouds scudding, like a train in the hands

of an unknown engineer drumming across tie
after tie. It's an enduring lack of silence, our
disintegration, like rain that drips onto one leaf

from another higher in the canopy, like the crows'
near-constant braggadocio. It's a sound
the possum in our woods ignores as she sleeps

under the brightened sky. But when she walks out
tonight, her pale stripped tail will shine in moonlight,
and trace behind her the places she has passed.

Entering the Earth

My father's forebears lie in a plot
overgrown with ferns and wild

blueberries: the only cemetery I like
to visit, though my husband's mother

once proclaimed it *unnatural,*
with no apparent irony. If a tombstone falls,

we let it be. The birds hear it,
like the echoes of caved-in mines

that killed so many of this graveyard's
earliest dead, those gritty

trussers of industrial democracy
who lived in darkness, working

the necessary magic of pulling coins
from earth. Only in highest summer –

the sun still above the horizon
when they surfaced, casting its bronze

over the lake – could they know light.
Or in their dreams, tinted

from pitch to walnut, singed
with copper, in veins like prayers

to follow deeper into the dark.

Christmas in Puerto Angel

By the time I saw it,
upside-down
between two men, wedged
into a rocky hollow
down-shore of the village,

blood from the first leg
was arcing toward me,
so much of it
and so much more red
than I could have imagined –
redder than hummingbirds,
than danger, than
my own heat –
four crimson flares
from the legs –

and one from the head,
left for last
as if to make the turtle
watch what I watched
from behind the rocks
behind the men
who ripped out the meat,
carried it away.

Around the shell
five scarlet ribbons –
slow red star exploding,
still moving
as circling gulls swooped in.

Snow Day

Everyone has stayed at home, snow
piling up like a photo-negative of night.

Suddenly everything essential yesterday
is less important than the fact of a roof

and a responsive thermostat. One person
sleeps in, sheet pulled up below his nose,

another stands at her living room window,
idly curious where hypnotism by snowflakes

might lead her. Across the street, a woman
hasn't even opened her drapes, plans to stay

in pajamas all day and indulge her sadness.
She can't name its origin, can only trace

its path tenderly as it meanders through her body
like a lost snake. She remembers it from deep

inside her childhood. *Good snake, dear snake* —
today interested in her ribs, weaving

in and out of them. Later, she will rise
abruptly, wrench her curtains open,

blink hard at the white blindness,
tell the snake to coil up and sleep.

Mourning Your Parents

The first time we sat in this field,
decades ago, fog rising from dew-dark grass,
the morning a single sheet of shimmer,
we softened our breathing to listen
to the river and you told me

how your father practiced
holding his breath, so many bad years
he lived through like that, so many
losses. How present death was –
your parents spoke often of it,
its ugliness, like a vacuum mounting
from their bellies to the crown of their heads,
fierce as earth's consumption of itself
by fire. Serafino, struck by lightning.
The twins. Leroy, at nine.

My family never spoke of death
except declawed, I told you then,
as a glimpse of something like
ascension, perfected perception.
You scoffed. *Flames burn real wounds,*
you pointed out. *It's abnormal*
not to acknowledge the ugly.

We won't be in this field again.
Your parents are dead, house and land
sold. You tell me: *I almost proposed to you*
that day. Rain begins to fall – large
soaking drops. *I was afraid when I should*
have been grateful. We stay put, huddled
on our log, welcome the drenching.

Thoughts Not My Own

They don't speak
but circle me and stare, as if
willing me to recognition.

Floating like swaying lanterns —
not what I know or can fathom,
phantoms of who I might be —

they are familiar and foreign.
I make out a shadow swathed in water
and weightless ribbons, a murmuring cloud

of lights like fireflies, a misted figure
strewing incantations like seed onto my bed
where you sleep beside me, love,

one arm thrown over your head,
mouth half-open, cheeks
inflating and collapsing beneath stubble.

The lanterns are dimming. You stir,
startled by your own sudden snoring,
and when you open your eyes

I tell you I crave your otherness.
You don't know what to say to that
but roll over to hold me.

The ghosts linger.

What You Listen To
2003

When the great blue heron lifted
from the pond behind the newlyweds
exchanging vows, I half-expected
the assembled guests and trees and geese

to break into a hymn and rise beside
the bird into the evening thickening
with cold and the absence of wind. Instead
no-one even gestured or gasped. So much

depends on what you listen to: promises,
or the slow beat, beat of wings pressing against
air. I remembered the heron when I stood
under a giant wind turbine in Okinawa, its whoosh

of blades driven by winds from China, my blood
rushing in sync with it, and I thought how we fight
hard to live, even the Iraqi child with half
a skull looking at me through her one eye

in the glossy red pictures my Japanese friend
showed me in despair and all I could say was
watashi-mo, wakarimasen,
I don't know, I don't understand either.

In my dreams, there's time to prepare for
earthquakes, and it's easy – just overturn
your belongings, as if the earth won't bother
with anything that seems already to have given up –

but no-one knows what's coming even though
we make pledges to eternity, and physicists
in silk tattersall ties insist we're approaching
a theory of everything. When the ceremony ended,

we shivered two by two up the garden path away
from the pond and the descent of night,
toward cake, dance music, and bowls
heaped with dripping, scarlet strawberries.

Black Magnolias

The black ones, says the customer. *The flowers.*
Magnolias, offers the clerk. *Those are magnolias,*
and I walk out the post office door

trying to imagine the stamps. I'm not
even sure what magnolias look like;
it's "Sugar Magnolia" that comes to mind,

guitar-cadenced, crystal-encrusted,
wide lips of petals perpetually opening, like
a sinkhole of desire, approach of a mirror,

reproach of my face that becomes
steadily less familiar, less sweet,
with the layers peeled back.

Black magnolias. Repulsive. Alluring.
How can you not want to lean into them,
thrill to the rotting? They bloom, I think,

on the very edge of the back-country,
like a thin inked contour line between town
and not-town, between the appearance

of refinement and the land that is done
with second-guessing its own nature.
They bloom where the river gets on

with flowing, confident of its destination.
I envy the magnolias this, how they drop themselves
flake by flake into the water and regret

nothing. And the thinnest flow becomes
a black torrent – something else I envy.
How the rivers keep emptying themselves

of all that darkness. Even if there's always
more coming, they let it go. Even the aging
magnolias, petal by sweet black petal.

Toccata

Tócame, the touch of your hand on my cheek
like a brush with something wild that lives
on the other side of the world, that lives

at the far end of my own depth, in the inky distances
of my mouth that I take you into. *Tócame*,
and I'll swallow the flecks in your eye

that gazes into me, the grey-green field
and the brown birds scattered on it, warm
like chocolate that melts into my breath,

melts onto my fingers. I'll smear you
with the dark exuding fluid of my dreams,
its heat, its redness – no, thicker than red,

slow and molten. This is how we levitate,
not just in dreams, but as we walk on earth –
beneath us, mountains churning, fire circling,

endless turmoil, white-hot. Touch
the earth: merciful crust cooled just enough
to hold us as we walk, as children walk to school,

trusting the next step to keep us in the air,
keep us where the rain can graze us, past
this umbrella discarded by the road, spokes

broken at useless angles and the black
sun-faded nylon flopping like a sail
intended for night but exposed. Oh,

how I do, oh how I don't wish to be seen –
so much dark inside me, and my buoyancy
only by grace of its heat.

Tócame, my love, touch the dark of me.

Light

When the lights went out
each night

I vanished like smoke
into an emptiness that spun

as nothing had ever spun before, ever –
new again now, and now, and now again –

where everything clamored, even
the last silence too far ahead to be seen

and there was no knowing me,
no way of naming me.

But when vision returned
in the morning

I undid my death. Yellow light suffused
the corner of a bedroom under a slanted ceiling.

Rain sheeted onto a patio below.
Everything continued.

Later, on an urban street I played in clogs
under tall towers of apartments

with rectangular windows, and though
I didn't understand the games, I played until

one by one each of us was called –
Pepe! Lucita! Lisken! –

and we vanished into the echoes of our names,
passing out of the streetlight's circumference and into

a dark river that circled us, a moat
whose crossing I remember

as a kind of breath-holding, like driving past
cemeteries in the family car, the same uncertainty

of emergence – and I wondered
who was the last child left and

how long would she wait for her name?

Death's Shadow

He keeps his shadow in this valley
of damp earth looped
from mountain ridges, moss
on downed hemlocks,
acorns, beetles, fern spores.

He has learned the grief of trees,
blends his shadow with theirs
cast against the sky. As the land turns
from the sun they climb together
like the prow of a boat lifting
and he can see everywhere.

When they creep back down in the morning
whole swaths of valley are bright
with beech leaves fallen like beacons
or gold coins minted from light,
and the faces of his dreams are obliterated.

He scatters his shadow into the gorge —
dark murmurs under stones,
trout ready to take the hook
he drops into the deepest place.

The Hubble Effect

for HPVP

In a life, the holes.

Parallel lives, where you were born a boy,
your blood didn't surprise you,
your grandfather didn't dive
into an empty swimming pool.

Places you didn't stay
filled with your absence,
ghosts of your footprints
finding their way like small iguanas
who have left their tails behind

on grey cracked pavement,
mown sward,
crumbling gravel –

so much abandoned
in an accelerating universe and still
we get larger.

We bring our absences with us –
spaces we didn't occupy,
comets we dreamed of touching,
notes we might have heard
had we flown
in another direction.

We're large as distance,
worlds in our ears,
our afterquakes like repercussions
spreading into places no-one

(not one of us, nothing)

has been before.

III

Fifth Essence

The Lure of the Exotic

It turns out the universe
isn't turquoise after all.

Rather it's a dull beige
and the scientist is apologizing
ruefully for getting us so
excited. This is the latest
in the scientific community.

He pooled all the light
in the observable universe, gathered it
into a computer, hit *mix*,
enter, came up
glorious blue-green

until he checked (belatedly,
in the interests of scientific rigor)
the color balance settings,
found programming errors,
had to settle for, well,
beige. Call it écru, if you wish,
or even fawn —

it's still no substitute
for the gleam of seas
deepening in twilight,
for gems scattered on our path,
for the promise we had swallowed:

we were made
(*how else could it be?*)
of splendor.

M-Theory

Fossils beneath me unstring themselves –
their spirals and gravitons

music made palpable

like a sleeve inflated on the clothesline,
afterburn of a plucked note –

vibrating earth
so thick with song

I can stand on it.

Five Strata of Here

I

Green wheeze of crickets aspiring
to ignition, and wind
combing pollen into the air.
Hedge roses smoldering and petals
scattered like bones picked clean.

II

Bottles, nails, a heavy
flat-iron, segments of old
railroad ties. Strap sandals.
And earthworms making the best of it.

III

Rutted road. Half-moons
from horseshoes. The snap
of a crop – a lady is waiting
up at the house where tea
will be served while evening settles
into a murmur. Here,
a knuckle bled into the ground
when it scraped against a stirrup.

IV

Very thin, very dense: a hard winter or two. Dark
with all the windows sealed. One suspects the memory
of daffodils in springtime, but the evidence is sparse.

V

Fires here. And an old forest.
Flicker of bone whittled
sharp: the shape of survival.
A cricket's wing in maple sap.

When the Fireflies Come Out

Right now it's still winter – waterfalls muted below ice, singe
of sun and earth's core equally out of range, fireflies unheated
like faded stars. Hand over hand days will pass like beads on a rosary,
until June, when we will seek fields of matted grasses, warming
roadsides, culverts below bridges, and will swear we see whole
constellations fallen. I am a clumsy hulk to their neat wings, precision
flashing, yet I answer to their signals. If I listen hard,
I can almost hear the lights click on and off. I never thought
to wonder where they winter, their fires smoldering under snow,
nestled in thistle root, larvae wriggling to the tremor of fox-tread
or pigeon-hoots. I hadn't even thought of them for months, until
today a young boy mentioned them. My birthday is when the
fireflies come out, he said. My breath caught in the jar of my chest.

You In This Field, Where I Have
Pulled Over My Bike

A bird with a fanned tail flurries a shrub
and two crows groom each other.
Stopping, I listen for what's there,
piccolo calls, maraca tree-tops.
The sky seems like absence but is full,
carries me in its furious journey,
sweeps bike, birds, trees into new days
weighty and sudden, each of us wayward
like so many unmatched balls to be juggled.
I am by this field, or in fern-nestled forest,
or – *and* – at the edge of a darkening beryl sea.
The wind sings to its destination, even
sings this field into a place inside me
that can be everywhere at once
and can make homes from ferns, sand
and the watchful assurance of crows.

Becoming Double

A number of us had gathered
in the curious way the world has
of gathering people, a random
rightness hovering, and then

what we all hoped for
though we could not name it,
sunshine in the dry altitude,
and conversation, and silence
resonant with a depth that made us
listen as if to reach the bottom of it.

At night the moon
scoured the hills and terraces.
Day warmed slowly. We followed
goat tracks up until we reached
a spring, its drinking trough filthy
with horseshit and roiled mud.
We stopped to watch a kestrel dive,
traded stares and greetings
with leathery goat-drivers on horseback,
scaled rocks like steps
to the top of the dusty hill-side.

One hill rose higher still.
The sign said *Propiedad Privada* but
the barbed wire was mostly trampled
horizontal. This was open land.
We walked into the sky.

This much is accurate.
What happened next
cannot be described so simply.
I too would have thought it impossible:
we reached the top but kept walking,
higher, as if we could fly by striding.

The hill that had seemed so tall
dropped away from us, flap
of wind-whipped ribbons
on huge crosses falling inaudible,
goat-bells paling. I saw
the wind itself rise to lift us.
In the distance the town grew smaller.

To this day I don't know
how we returned or even if
we came back to the same land
we had left. Dust still clings
to my boots and hawks
still call sharply at the sight of prey.
The sun rises each morning
and the moon cycles.
A number of us depart
and reunite. Two are me.

Tommy

I didn't know about your heart
when I met you on the ferry
and fell in love with you

beguiled by your two great
wagging St. Bernards.
I was eight. You were fifteen

and still had four good years
before you'd lie down
near some railway tracks in Michigan,

set your clock for six
and close your book –
Portrait of the Artist as a Young Man.

When they found you, I
was just beginning adolescence
but knew already that love

is unmistakable, that it is old,
that it trembles with one particular
frequency, as if you and I

and all the others I have loved
are one soul scattered
in many bodies.

We were both freckled,
said little, just grinned a lot
and introduced our families.

Now, when I ride a ferry
I walk around it
once, alone –

feel for the engines' thrum
in the handrails, listen
to the ocean beating back.

The Lake Isn't a Life

but it understands
being forgotten,
has learned to remember itself —

slow heavy depths,
      the overflow of night,
            earth's confidante.

Not a color either —
what we call *blue, green*
but a tone outside the spectrum —

liquefied light,
      sky poured into furrows,
            cold secret currents.

It's stubborn —
won't stop hammering the rocks,
stirring the land —

mottled dream residue,
      the aftershock of rain,
            my breath made molten.

Air

What we can't see, can't smell, can't taste, can't hold,
can't do without.

The rest of it: what we throw away.
Superfluous gases. Dust, pollen,
exhaust.

What we see when we look
up. What we imagine
awaits us. Where we locate
most of our gods.

A great unfillable void, as in all
that has disappeared *into thin air.*

Breeze with the brazen smell
of plant sex, their flower-commerce, or of
salt drying, or hot dogs and pretzels.

What lets my molecules become your
molecules, what they travel through.

What we give to our grievances.

Where we go to share news or express opinions.
The time to do so.

What we put on when we feel least at ease, some of us.
False pride, or any impression we render
as aura: confidence, diffidence, regret.
How we carry our particular burdens.

A melody. Something that floats to us
from across a meadow.
Something that plays in our ear
and remains.

Relief. Coolness in summer, as in *air conditioning*.
Space to think, as in *give me some air*.

What we breathe.
The breath itself.
What we share.

Everything between.

The Latch Once Lifted

Light opens, vertical
like your body, your
shape but growing
and glowing as who would not
want to – so
you are willing
to risk desert, the scorch
of it, its lack
of hiding places.
You'll be a lizard
surviving
in a dry arroyo,
each yesterday washed away
by flooding light.

Keeping My Eyes Up

When I was seven and ardent for official status
as a Safe Bicycle Rider, I feared failure
at staying on the straight line until Daddy advised
keeping my eyes up, looking far into the future.
I rode directly towards it, jubilant.

Today, I rose at dawn for a first ride
in a brand-new landscape: discovered
nothing but grey-white sky draped over morning.

So I guessed at hills still covered, their heft
and contours, conjured whole ranges
at the end of the white line I rode on,
reveling, as usual, in the occluded –
a mountain ridge set to reveal itself,

an ice cream truck sure to be just around the corner.
Back then, I rang my handle-mounted bell
over and over, pressed my thumb hard
into the contoured metal, announced
my pure delight in what was coming.

This morning, I watched it clear slowly
from north to south, my faith soon to be rewarded:
where I'd envisioned mountains –
blue clear to the horizon, wide open.

On Not Unfurling My Wings

I'm not saying I'm an angel.
It's just that I have wings - ghost-wings
that grow from my shoulders,
like limbs an amputee knows
to be present despite the evidence.

They're strong, masterful, not something
I asked for, but despite their weight
I've grown used to them,
would miss them.

They don't take up much room, folded,
and I don't unfurl them in company.

At a party the other night, a rainbow
threw itself against the long ridge opposite,
and everyone stopped talking,
turned to the east, and gazed —

a small moment of glory,
the unseen made manifest.

My wings burned.

Mathematics of the Impossible

I step barefoot through the quiet
groves inside me, learn
that love waits in the clearings

where I find myself again.

The wind rushing through me slows,
an invisible bird sings its rapture.
The sky vibrates in response, and my glade

expands, as if with breath,
more and more openness inside me.

Beyond dimension –

x for pine-scent or the taste of ripeness,
y for the warmth of sun.

Deer emerge from shadows into light.
It's not a safe place, but
it is a place of sustenance.

Salt, cedar, and sinew equal z.
z is equal to more than its sum –
the blue of the Aegean beyond the spectrum,
what soars in a melody

that's unexplained by theory.
I begin to understand the scale of love's sphere.
Neither north nor south. Not east or west.

And the clearing widens again.

Particle Physics

I want to give you all I have known —

       whispering grasses, gods
       sleeping in ridged clouds,

       the weight of purple
       when lilacs die or when night

           grows into itself —

We are becoming something
else, you and I —

           I want to move you, I want to move you —

Hear how the world is singing

ringing

flinging

       itself through us —

           we,
           mostly nothing but space.

This River as One

Lick your palms: you'll taste it, your
ocean nature fooled into a narrow course

like my precious river here. It's not
difficult to imagine it as one

with all the other rivers, all molecules shared:
what's Orinoco now the Loire next week,

the Mississippi's roil flown in from China's Yangtze,
what's warm once cold, what's salty soon dried

free of sediment – not quite the sleight
of transubstantiation, but still, you get the point

if you keep going back, from flood to stream
to drop, to atom, quark, and spirit. If you go

small enough, even the hard among us:
invisible, passed through like liquid, easy.

IV

From a Distance

The Edge of Everything

Mark how the straw chatters,
thrashed by the wind.

Your own voice has withered
into the flickering of a small grass-snake,

larynx left opening and closing
in a perpetual imminence of sound.

Here is the edge of everything:
field, forest, night,

the intention of understanding.
Ahead of you, a palace

thrusting unsupported terraces into the air, or else
the denial of all you have ever said.

Your signature is etched into a maple leaf
somewhere in these woods,

or carved in the deep loam
riddled with earthworms under your feet.

It is up to you to decide
whether to proceed or to return.

Hyacinths bloom here now. Come fall,
they will consume themselves again.

In Both Hands

Like one of the Magi bearing gifts,
for two nights in a row I have shown up
with a turtle, and no good reason for it,
no one to give it to. Even in the dreams
I have been puzzled, cradling the creature
in both hands, its mottled carapace
domed like a miniature arc of Earth
tessellated with tectonic plates. Well,
it drifted to me somehow, and so
I carry it, and have nothing to say
to those who question me about it.
Exploration is an act of will initially
but then you just have to take what you get
and tend it, from favorite coffee mug
to high wind sponging the sky grey
on grey. Even the neighbor yelling
at his dogs – or his wife – is a gift,
something that belongs to this life only.
I don't remember if my turtle
stuck his head out from his roof
but I think he must have. I think
it was me with the closed eyes: I called
Marco! and his voice answered *Polo!*
Polo! and when I found him I brushed
pollen from his shell into the breeze
and I brought the turtle with me
wherever I was going, surprised
at how little a life weighs
though it fills up both my hands.

No One Counting

Wave-ward, and wave-fro, reef-bound
and barracuda-drawn, strong rasp
of in-snorkel, out-snorkel, before silence

of a dive, and this the fear of it, breath
stopped and what is vague now between me
and the air, distant. This is a wildness

I am not part of, though I pretend –
world without play, world where *to be*
is *to survive* – and beneath in the channel

deeper than visibility allows
larger creatures pass as on a highway,
silent-slicing, masters of seeing

without being seen. After, from the boat,
sound – like pebbles scattering,
wrasses arc out of their element

in a silver waterfall away from something
that threatens them, the sea turtle,
or something bigger, and no one

counting, no one to miss any one of them
when it is gone, no one to miss
any one of them, gone.

Visiting the Burn Unit

for jJ

1

Who hasn't been seduced by a campfire,
its lust for oxygen,
its lick, its hiss, its color-coded heat.

But that's not this story.

> *Put on a gown and gloves before you enter the patient's room.*
> *If you leave, even for a moment, put on a new gown and new gloves*
> *when you return.*

This story is bare feet in the street
and nothing in your hand
but a remote mistaken for a phone
when you woke to flames eating the kitchen
and the power out –

> *Behave as each staff member requires you to behave.*
> *This goes for the patient also.*

My cat! Find my cat! you begged the firemen.

> *Do not allow the patient to drink water.*
> *She needs calories to rebuild her skin.*

Lisken, you say, as if confiding a secret: the flames
were beautiful.

> *Patient can aid healing by elevation and movement.*

You dance with your hands in the air.

2

Face blotched with blisters and raw skin,
hair shaved back and singed,

> *Patient has mid- and deep-dermal burns*
> *over approximately 18% of her body (using rule of nines);*

both arms swathed like a mummy's in white gauze.

> *Patient will require hospitalization, debridement*
> *of devitalized tissue, and possibly skin grafts.*

Knowing nothing, I was braced for worse.
Still —

> *Patient should be monitored for burn wound conversion:*
> *it may be a week or more before the wounds fully reveal themselves.*

As if the fire were still smoldering in your flesh.

3

Back home, I climb Monument Mountain
to a view of parallel ridges,
a horizon announcing *elsewhere*.

> *Do not expect us to explain everything.*

I am out of breath.

It will take time for us to know everything.
It may also be in your best interests not to know everything.

So much existence at once.

Do not say burn victim. Say burn survivor.

My eye focuses further and further.
You are far to the west.

Beautiful, you'd told me: the colors,
and on such a scale.

Lineage

Twelve generations ago a man
with your name stepped onto America
and it was days before the ground

stopped rocking, but he strode on
westward and procreated
in the new land full of sky and

migrations. In your dream
another man with your name
flies between two women on wings

more like a crow's than a butterfly's,
until the morning whirr of the coffee grinder
wakes you. Over coffee you read

about a small oil spill and wonder
if it will make national news and if
you could get your name cited

by rescuing a loon or
staging a one-person rally in favor
of self-sufficiency, like the time

you streaked in Zermatt
in an inebriated ritual to banish
fog from the Matterhorn, only

the Swiss media paid no attention,
your only satisfaction
from a Brit muttering *bloody*

brave, bloody brave over raclette
and Riesling. He shook your hand
and said goodbye almost mournfully,

reminding you of the stray dog years before
that materialized from deep Maine darkness
and trotted beside you all the way

to the highway where you left him
for a ride and he howled after you.
When you get up from the breakfast table,

you go out to the garden and harvest
leeks which you offer to your wife
like long-stemmed roses

and she accepts them
and kisses you and whispers
your name.

West Stockbridge, 1941

for MLD, in memoriam

When the whistle blew
not at noon
all the wives billowed out

into the street and peered
south towards the quarry,
squinting, breathing in

flour brushed from aprons.
Someone was hurt, maybe
even dead. You don't remember

which – only that your man
came home right away,
laid down his pick-axe

and hugged you
there in the road,
covering you with limestone.

Abundance

I have woken without regrets
into a dawn of chardonnay light

creeping into the valley.
Everything I own is in this morning

and I have left it unlocked.
Look, on scree you can still balance

as you slide down the mountain
and you have lost nothing,

having received the views toward which
your back was turned

on the ascent: the shape of the copse
from which you set out,

and the water in the cove
a color beyond depth,

and the small mottled bird
foraging in tall grasses

since before you began.
They are not necessary

but they are the life you've been offered.
I am trembling open

as light trembles
at both dawn and dusk.

Beach Drawing, Age 8

The dunes loomed enormous. Now I stand
on the same shore – sawgrass at my feet,

sand smoothed as if strewn for my arrival,
low rolling rumble of the sea –

and see the beach both as it is
and as it appeared then, felt-tipped with vigor.

Dense stripes of green, yellow, and blue
filled the page, no white paper anywhere.

My mother framed the picture, hung it
by the kitchen window above the chair

I perched on as we talked about my day
(my endless chatter, her interjections, nods).

Suddenly I feel the people we were then –
the child, the woman younger than I am now –

like totems somewhere inside me, like spirits.
I am moved by the surge and pull of their reach,

by their minnow flutterings. They nose
at the soft spots inside me, like the water

on this shore laps sand into pleats.
I've come here with no particular agenda

but have discovered a kitchen bright with sunlight
and the clatter of saucepans. Nothing here is sought,

only found: the wet-dry zippered boundary,
the gulls and crabs, the spume between them.

My mother praised the perspective,
said I'd understand later.

The Language of Flight

Nuthatches, a woodpecker, and chickadees
weave aerial signatures across the yard
like messages from another time that is

                                        not ours,

not the hour that holds us in the small
incision of its grace
                        and because they are
from another time I can't read them: they
require a quicker eye or a tongue that shapes
differently, a tongue that hears.

                                Mine
understands only honey and salt; my tongue
licks honeysuckle blossoms and drops them,
oblivious to the sound of their decay.

Even in the present
                        I speak imperfectly.

So what am I to do
                        when a wren wheels
into the maple above my head and another
unseen bird thrashes in the hands of the ash
tree's paling leaves:

                        they are dancing
across a bluing sky, through air of no
color at all.

If you were here, who's heard
songs fall for so many years, perhaps
you could tell me what the script means,
perhaps you could translate.

                           But what
would it gain us, both unable to interpret
how our own paths have spiraled,
what our two flights express. So many

things we each can say.
                      But not that.

Flight of Starlings

From the bay window in our living room
it looks like dozens of starlings
have just flown into your workshop below me,

dive-bombers launched from the trees
to the snow-free ground under our eaves.
I imagine them in there, winging

among the tools, perched on the table saw
or pecking at jars of screws and wall plugs.
One loses a feather. When you come home

you'll find a filigree of spindly footprints
in the sawdust, and the black iridescence
of the bird's absence. It is something

utterly other, this feather, this bird.
It's from another place, and anyone who says
you can go there is a liar – it can't happen

any more than we can go back
to a time before loss. But somewhere
a bird is balancing effortlessly on a branch

or in the air, without that feather.

Sister's Son

Remember we were in Paris, you say again,
when William was born? Yes! It was March,
rainy and cold, and we were borrowing

someone's apartment – well, renting,
but it felt like borrowing –
our upstairs neighbors alternately fighting

and fucking above our bed, wet walks
from the métro hauling cheese, bread,
pains au chocolat for breakfast, our struggle

through the passage to the mildewed stairs,
impossible not to knock paint off the plaster
as we squeezed past someone coming down.

Half a world away in Ohio my sister
waited to give birth, and we waited
for her call, past due. In the evenings,

we'd dodge rush-hour pedestrians and walk
the back way to the Bistro Renard, where
we always had the eldest waiter, impeccably

professional but still you told me
you felt we did something wrong –
elbows or our hands, or tipping, or drinking

the wrong water. Later, after one last
glass of wine, we'd fall asleep clutching
each other as if afraid, though we were free

of all requirements, even of our own lives
in this Marais flat, with its orange rug
and glass table and tall drapes pulled back

from a drafty window overlooking
the central courtyard shaft. We made
our bed daily, and my nephew

finally arrived. Now when we say,
Remember we were in Paris when William was born?
our memory of his birth has a sheen

as if he were quicksilver or we were overflowing
into the world, our love too much
for a single place, though we found

the stairwell a little frightening,
and the sheets, for all their softness,
belonged to someone else.

Broken Things

(for Benjamin Bright Ladley)

When the boy fell, what
he saw: boulders, scree,

a delicate kestrel
in flight. The sky, this

earth, how it breaks apart,
the urge to shatter.

Moon-splinter behind a tower.
What he heard: church bells

counting cormorants black
against the dawn,

bleat of a hungry goat, roar
of a plane pressed into air.

In his pocket, stones.
A piece of blue tile.

What she remembers: his palm
on the nape of her neck,

her fingers on his cock,
red ache like magma welling

from the earth's core.
What we share with the other side,

take in, mix, can't hold:
tears, juices, lava

of our loneliness, cells shed
into each other's hands.

Seam

Our heads thrown back and arcing
with the sound above –

      wing-thuds of cormorants –

a line of them horizon to horizon,
a seam, moving –

      here day,
            here night –

not dark, light
but one side or the other
of cormorants

         who know
when it is time to move

      from this water
      to that, wing-tip
            to wing-tip

over the red-brown city waking,
      cold shadows, pigeons shifting,

through morning sky, fresh pool
of forever, blue field of the unattainable –

what is there to grasp, nothing
      to close my fist on –

                        and the line

passes over us and we lose
sight of them

and look at each other

            as if there were something
            waiting to be said.

Recall

Once he knew rhetoric,
apologia his specialty

> *Now I forget*
> *the smell of fennel and*
> *the uses of time*

He understood his own brain,
its cortex and networks

> *See — it is fretted with dew*
> *each time I wake to it*
> *How the colors run and shimmer!*

He believed in reciprocity
and just desserts

> *Do as you would*
> *Others do unto you*
> *Have unto them*

Mercy —

> Push, and the tide goes out, the shore
> opening its eye to a wide gaze
> taking in the sky, wind-paddled
> and bright, the foamy retreating
> edge of the ocean, the stranded
> life — kelp, sea-purses, drying crabs.

It is not a matter of pity.
It is a rare gift to be
in the eye of a true beholder.

Pull, and a mountain rises,
grey miracle of crystal engineering.
Gneiss. Granite. And an afternoon
that goes on forever.

In God's encyclopedia, he thinks,
(he likes to think of God's encyclopedia)
water is the childhood of evolution.

It's a salty theology,
brine crusty but beautiful.

And look there — the moon
nothing but cloud.

On Needing Glasses

Perhaps it will be easier
without them, at the end,
the world having faded
gradually. Friends' features
forgotten ahead of time,
clouds receded, color smudged –
all detail blurred into a white
thickening like the funnel
of this rock-wall spider's web
I peer into, straining to focus
on the vanishing point.

Made in the USA
Middletown, DE
26 April 2016